LIGHTHOUSES

LIGHTHOUSES

JENNY LINFORD

p

This is a Parragon Publishing Book
First published in 2006

Parragon Publishing
Queen Street House
4 Queen Street
Bath, BA1 1HE, UK

Produced by Atlantic Publishing

All photographs courtesy of Corbis
(except the illustration on page 13 which was kindly supplied
by the Trustees of the National Museums of Scotland)
Text © Parragon Books Ltd 2006

ISBN 1-40547-117-4
Printed in China

CONTENTS

INTRODUCTION

From our earliest history, mankind has used light and fire to fight the darkness. Warning beacons on hill-tops, blazing through the night, have given notice of impending attack. Perhaps this fundamental, powerful fact has contributed to our continuing fascination with lighthouses, which, even in the 21st century, still illuminate the dark, offering guidance to those at sea.

An archetypal image of a lighthouse consists of a simple, tall, white tower, with a bright beam streaming out from its lantern. The reality is far more various and fascinating. Visit Bremerhaven in Germany, famous for its "forest" of lighthouses, and one will find romantic, nineteenth-century Gothic-inspired creations as well as modern, functional towers. In France, Cordouan, dating back to 1611, is a refined and elegant stone tower, housing a richly decorated interior complete with a Royal Chapel. The Statue of Liberty, erected in 1886, one of the world's most recognizable monuments, was initially a lighthouse (the responsibility of the U.S. Lighthouse Board from its erection in New York Harbor until 1901). Furthermore, it was the first lighthouse in America to use electricity, with light blazing out from Lady Liberty's upraised torch. Canada's classic "pepperpot" lighthouses, with their tapered square base pyramid shape, the Florida Keys' screwpile towers in the middle of the sea, Iceland's distinctive bright orange, squat lighthouses (colored for maximum visibility against the snow), a pretty Greek temple-like lighthouse on Cephalonia – these all serve the same purpose, yet each is deliciously different from the other, a tribute to man's ingenuity.

HISTORY OF LIGHTHOUSES

The world's first true lighthouse was a splendid one: the great Pharos at the port of Alexandria. So remarkable was this construction that it was deemed one of the Seven Wonders of the Ancient World, the only one of the seven to have a practical purpose. Authorized by Egypt's ruler Ptolemy Soter in 290 B.C. and completed around 270 B.C. during the reign of Ptolemy II, the building was erected on the island of Pharos, after which it was named, and was designed to lead shipping safely into Alexandria's busy port.

The architect of this extraordinary building was one Sostrates, whose dedication on the tower read: "Sostrates, the son of Dexiphanes of Knidos, dedicated this to the Savior Gods on behalf of those who sail the sea". The story goes that Ptolemy II demanded that the lighthouse be dedicated to him so Sostrates first had his personal dedication chiseled into the foundations, then a dutiful dedication to Ptolemy II carved into the plaster coating on top. With the passing of time, the plaster chipped and fell away revealing Sostrates's hidden dedication to the world.

At the time of construction the building was one of the tallest structures in the world, surpassed only by the Great Pyramids. Coated in white marble, it must have been a truly impressive sight. According to ancient accounts the Pharos Lighthouse was 300 cubits tall. With the cubit varying in length from country to country, it is thought today that the tower stood an impressive 450–600 ft high. It was constructed in three stages; the first stage at the base was square, the second octagonal and the third circular, with the light on the top of the circular tower. Apparently the Pharos Lighthouse was lit with a bonfire at night but used a large mirror, possibly made of polished metal, to reflect the sun's rays during the day. Legend has it that the huge mirror was used to detect enemy ships and to set them alight. In clear conditions the light at its pinnacle could be seen from some 30 miles away. Damaged by earthquakes over the centuries, the Pharos Lighthouse was in ruins by A.D. 1349 and in A.D.1480 a fort was built on its ruined foundations.

To this day, however, the Pharos Lighthouse has left a significant inheritance. So synonymous was the great structure at Alexandria with lighthouses that the word for lighthouse in a number of languages comes from Pharo, with "phare" being French for lighthouse, and "faro" Spanish and Italian for lighthouse. Indeed, the science of lighthouse construction is known as "pharology."

The Romans valued lighthouses and during the Roman Empire many were constructed around Europe. Dover Castle contains the ruins of an 80-ft-high lighthouse tower, while Boulogne in France was home to the famous Tour d'Ordre, commissioned by the Emperor Caligula in A.D.40. On Spain's Atlantic coast the striking La Coruna lighthouse is the longest-serving lighthouse in the world, dating back to Roman times. Following the collapse of the Roman Empire around A.D. 500, maritime trade declined and the lighthouses fell into disrepair.

During the Middle Ages in Europe, coastal monasteries and chapels often lit warning beacons to guide mariners. Portugal's oldest lighthouse, Cabo de Sao Vicente, dates back to a monastery built in 1515 on the site on which the monks lit a fire. The Benedictine monks at St. Michael's Mount in Cornwall, England, whose priory there was built in 1135, shone a light from a tower to guide local fishermen. The dissolution of the monasteries in England in the 1530s saw the end of many of these lights. In 1513, however, King Henry VIII of England had granted a charter to the Guild of the Blessed Trinity "so that they might legislate the pilotage of ships in the king's streams." Over the following centuries, Trinity House began constructing lighthouses, though many were privately built and run. In 1836 all private lights in England, Wales, and the Channel Islands were placed under the management of Trinity House and the organization continues to manage these today.

Opposite: Old Head of Kinsale, County Cork, Ireland.

The rise of the mercantile powers during the eighteenth and nineteenth centuries, together with industrial advances, saw lighthouses develop around the world, with countries including France, America, and Britain realizing the importance of constructing them and also developing the technology with which to do so. Shipping was such a hazardous affair that in 1800 it was estimated that one ship was lost or wrecked around the British coast every day. Pioneering lighthouse engineers, such as Robert Stevenson, often faced hostility from the remote seashore communities who profited from the wrecks and had no wish to see them cease. Despite the obstacles of bureaucratic indifference, funding problems, political inertia, and considerable engineering difficulties, lighthouses were built around the world, providing sailors not only with warning lights but an invaluable navigation tool.

CONSTRUCTING LIGHTHOUSES

The history of lighthouses is filled with notable examples of formidable obstacles being overcome. The earliest lighthouses were constructed on the shore, but all too often the real need was for lighthouses out at sea. By their nature, lighthouses, especially those at sea, were sited in the most dangerous waters, surrounded by treacherous reefs.

The first permanent lighthouse to be built offshore was off England's southern coast during the seventeenth century. With Plymouth (from whence the Pilgrim Fathers set sail) increasingly important as a port, the need to warn sailors of the notorious Eddystone reef fourteen miles off

the coast became more and more urgent. Inventor and shipowner Henry Winstanley (1644–1703), having himself lost ships on Eddystone's dangerous rocks, decided to construct a lighthouse on the reef, a feat which was popularly thought to be impossible. In order to build the light, Winstanley and his crew found themselves working on rocks which were almost fully submerged at high tide, making conditions hazardous and progress slow. To add to his woes, Winstanley was captured by a French privateer, though fortunately released on the orders of the French King Louis XIV who, on learning what Winstanley was trying to do, declared "France was at war with England not with humanity."

On November 14, 1698, Winstanley's wooden lighthouse was completed and fishermen returned to Plymouth with the astonishing news that Eddystone was showing a light. In the face of carping critics who

Below: The battle to construct the world's first permanent offshore lighthouse at Eddystone saw a number of valiant attempts, including Winstanley's and Rudyerd's wooden lighthouses. It was John Smeaton's pioneering stone design, however, which solved many of the engineering problems inherent in such a project.

Opposite: The invention by Augustin Jean Fresnel in 1822 of the Fresnel Lens revolutionized lighthouse lamps. The Fresnel lens used prisms to gather and concentrate light from its source, so producing a far more powerful beam of light than any lantern had previously generated.

warned that his lighthouse would not survive the winter, Winstanley declared that he wanted to be in his lighthouse during England's greatest storm. Unfortunately for him his wish was granted. In November 1703, Winstanley went out to the Eddystone light to oversee repairs. While he was there England experienced the Great Storm of 1703, of which Daniel Defoe wrote: "No pen could describe it, nor tongue express it, nor thought conceive it unless by one in the extremity of it." In the morning, the Eddystone Lighthouse and its creator had disappeared.

The continuing saga of the Eddystone Lighthouse is a tribute to human perseverance. A second wooden lighthouse was constructed six years later, which was to last an impressive 46 years. This was destroyed by a blaze in 1755 and, horribly, the 94-year-old lighthouse keeper Henry Hall, while looking up at the melting roof swallowed molten lead and died a few days later.

It was the pioneering engineer John Smeaton (1724–92), regarded today as the founder of civil engineering in Britain, who solved many of the engineering problems that a lighthouse in such an exposed position faced. Famously, he announced that he would seek inspiration from the strong oak tree which can withstand gales, by constructing a broad-based stone tower that tapered gradually towards the top.

Having assembled a crew of Cornish tin miners to cope with the arduous work in store, Smeaton's team set to work, building their 72-ft-high tower out of 1,493 granite blocks each dovetail-jointed to the next. In order to hold the tower together, Smeaton invented a quick-drying cement, essential in the wet conditions he was working in, a formula which is still in use today. Smeaton's Eddystone Tower was lit by 24 candles on October 16, 1759 and was a revolutionary breakthrough in lighthouse design, much-followed around the world. Although his lighthouse stood firm for many decades, cracks appeared in the rock on which it was built in the 1870s and the top half was dismantled. Its stump still stands there on Eddystone Rock, a lasting tribute to Smeaton's construction skills.

Today's Eddystone Lighthouse, constructed by James Douglass (1826–98) in 1882, drew both on Smeaton's original design and Robert Stevenson's work, to build a formidable stone structure, this time using larger blocks. Now automated, the Eddystone Lighthouse continues to warn shipping to this very day.

John Smeaton's success in constructing the Eddystone Lighthouse was to inspire Robert Stevenson (1772–1850), a pioneering figure in Scottish lighthouse construction. The Scottish coast offered many dangers to shipping, the most notorious being Bell Rock in the entrance to the Firth of

Forth. In 1799 over 70 ships were lost along that stretch of the coast and in 1800 Robert Stevenson, a young engineer working for the Northern Lighthouse Board, submitted a radical proposal to construct a lighthouse on Bell Rock itself. The board, however, balked both at cost and the difficulties inherent in the proposal and it took a major tragedy to focus attention on Bell Rock once more. In 1804 the 64-gun *H.M.S.York* was torn apart on Bell Rock, with the loss of 491 lives and finally, in 1806, the scheme was given the go-ahead, with John Rennie as chief engineer and Robert Stevenson as resident engineer.

The obstacles faced by Stevenson and his crew were formidable. Not only did Bell Rock stand 11 miles out to sea, but the rock was submerged by up to 16 feet of water for most of the day. Using a floating light and base vessel, Stevenson built a barrack on stilts on the Bell Rock reef where the workmen could stay and where materials could be brought to from the shore. Stevenson and his crew worked in unenviable, dangerous conditions, with chronic seasickness an added burden. They labored with pickaxes (as gunpowder might have damaged the fabric of the reef itself) constructing the tower out of horizontally dovetailed 1-ton granite blocks with no cement, and work progressed slowly as, because of the high waters, they were limited to a two-hour "window" each low tide. At one point, when their transport ship to the reef came adrift from its moorings, Stevenson and his men faced drowning by the rising tide but fortunately were rescued by the chance arrival of the mail boat. After two years' work, the tower stood only six feet tall, with 94 feet still to be constructed. Working doggedly away, however, the crew saw the tower completed and lit in February 1811. An impressive sight to this day, the Bell Rock Lighthouse is a tribute to Stevenson's skills, requiring not a single repair to its stonework. A target during World War II, it has survived not only being machine-gunned by a Geman plane but also a German bomb exploding on the rock some 30 feet from the lighthouse which amazingly left it unscathed.

Following his achievement at Bell Rock, Robert Stevenson went on to construct or design at least 25 Scottish lighthouses and founded a dynasty of Scottish lighthouse engineers, with his grandson, the writer Robert Louis Stevenson, justly proud of his engineering ancestors' enduring legacy. The Stevenson family were also to play their part in influencing the development of the lighthouse in Japan. David and Thomas Stevenson, of the Northern Lighthouse Board, recommended Scottish civil engineer Richard Henry Brunton (1841–1901) for the post of Chief Lighthouse Engineer to the Japanese government, a position he took up in 1868. In a remarkable eight-year period, Brunton supervised the construction of over 50 lighthouses around the Japanese coast and established a training school and system. The lighthouses Brunton constructed were all modeled on designs by the Stevenson family but had to be adapted to the fact that Japan is prone to earthquakes, with Brunton adding stabilizing bars and also constructing lighthouses totally of metal. In Japan he is known to this day as the "Father of Japanese Lighthouses."

Eddystone and Bell Rock offered models of construction which proved hugely influential around the world. Today, modern technology has taken away the need to build expensive new lighthouses and there is an emphasis on preservation. This too involves impressive feats of engineering, as the moving of Cape Hatteras Lighthouse on America's North Carolina coast amply demonstrates. An iconic lighthouse, the 208-ft tower, built in 1870, faced such severe coastal erosion that its future was in jeopardy. It was finally agreed to move the whole building away from the predatory ocean. This

Opposite: The Fresnel lamp at Yaguina Head Lighthouse, Oregon, USA.

project involved removing 800 tons from the tower's base, replacing them with steel supports equipped with hydraulic jacks. The tower was then lifted six feet off the ground, supported, and moved along on rollers. It began its journey on June 17, 1999 and arrived safely at its destination 1,600 feet from the sea on July 9, 1999 — yet another remarkable achievement in the annals of lighthouse engineering.

LIGHTHOUSE LIGHTS

From their early history, lighthouses had sought to project their light as far as possible. It was realized early on that, to compensate for the curvature of the earth, lights needed to be set as high as possible simply to be seen at any distance, hence the construction of lighthouse towers and the positioning of beacons on naturally high points such as cliffs or hills. For centuries, lighthouses were lit simply by fires. The only way to increase the brightness of the light was to build a larger fire, but fuel costs and the logistics of having large blazes on the top of lighthouses made this impractical. When oil lamps replaced candles, spermaceti oil, made from the blubber of the much-hunted sperm whale, was favored for its bright, even light (with the term "candle power" originating in the use of spermaceti candles). One step forward came with the invention in 1781 by Swiss chemist Aime Argand of a new lamp which cast a brighter light. Argand's lamp, plus reflectors, became widely used in European lighthouses. In 1812 in North America, Windsor Lewis patented a "reflecting and magnifying lantern" which had borrowed heavily from Argand's lamp and, despite the fact that it required constant cleaning and adjustment, the Lewis lamp was installed in most American lighthouses.

Lighthouse lamps were revolutionized by the work of French physicist Augustin Jean Fresnel (1788–1827), a pioneer in the field of optics, credited with discovering a number of optical formulas and fascinated by reflection and refraction. In 1822 Fresnel invented the intricate construction known as the Fresnel lens or dioptric lens, a convex lens surrounded by concentric rings of glass prisms, resembling a glass beehive. Whereas the previous parabolic reflector lights had transmitted 39 percent of the original light source, Fresnel's lens was able to efficiently collect and direct 80 percent, providing a far more powerful beam. Fresnel's ground-breaking lens was first tested in 1823 at the historic lighthouse at Cordouan; the light it produced was so bright that reputedly the locals thought that the tower was on fire. Sadly, Fresnel died in 1827 before seeing the extent to which his lens was taken up by lighthouses around the world. He left, however, a life-saving legacy which is still in use today.

One of the advantages of the Fresnel lens was that it could be used to send out either a constant light beam or a flashing beam. The latter, using flash and eclipse intervals, enabled lighthouses to have their "light characteristic", an individual flashing pattern which sailors could identify. The insertion of colored glass also allowed for different colored flashing lights to be transmitted, another aid in identification. A flashing light, incidentally, is far easier for a human eye to spot than a static one. The invention of the Fresnel lens, therefore, was part of the process by which lighthouses became an invaluable means of navigation as well as simply warning of shipping hazards.

In order to support these extremely heavy crystal lanterns and their optics and allow them to be revolved, it was necessary to find a mechanism that not only offered the least resistance but would also take up the smallest amount of space. Ingeniously, the revolving Fresnel lenses were, therefore, placed upon "mercury floats", pools of liquid mercury. With mercury 13.6 times heavier than water and able to support 35 times more weight by varied hugely in size, with smallest sixth order lenses being only two feet (0.6 m) high but the largest first order lens (consisting of over 1,000 prisms) standing a magnificent 12 feet (3.7 m) tall and 6 feet (1.8 m) across. In North America, the smaller lenses were used along lakes, inlets and harbors, with the large first, second and third lenses placed on the coast. North American lighthouses, however, were slow to benefit from Fresnel's breakthrough discovery. Stephen Pleasonton, the Fifth Auditor of the U.S. Treasury, was reluctant to even test the Fresnel lens and it was only when administration of aids to navigation was taken out of his hands and assigned to the U.S. Lighthouse Board in 1853 that Fresnel lenses were used throughout North America's lighthouses.

LIGHTHOUSE KEEPERS

Historically, lighthouse keepers have always occupied a special place in our collective imagination. With so many lighthouses located in bleak, remote places, one wonders at the character of someone who would choose to live in such isolated, and often hazardous, circumstances. Lighthouse keepers had either to cope with periods of total solitude or, perhaps worse, living in a confined space with one or two other people. This is work that must appeal to people who have little time for society, with the hermit Galfridus, who tended the lighthouse at Cordouan, the archetypal figure of a keeper. The fact that their work meant the difference between lives being saved or lost has always added both an importance and a certain glamor to their occupation. The American President Thomas Jefferson summed up the vital nature of their work when he declared: "I think the keepers of lighthouses should be dismissed for small degrees of remission, because of the calamities which even these produce."

A lighthouse keeper's duties obviously centered on the light. The lamp had to be lit at sunset every day and extinguished every morning at sunrise, with careful track kept of the oil consumed. During a night watch a keeper would have to check the light and wind the weights that rotated the light when necessary. Keeping the lens of the lamp and the windows clean was also important so as to ensure maximum visibility and was no mean feat. Trimming the burnt lamp wicks so that they didn't smoke and dirty the glass was such a big part of a keeper's job that in the States keepers were known as "wickies." Lighthouse keepers were also in charge of fog bells or horns and in foggy conditions the weights that worked these had to be wound every 2–4 hours. On top of that, the lighthouse tower and keeper's dwelling had to be maintained through carpentry and painting. Lighthouse logs, where the keepers had to keep a record of weather conditions and the work done, record a daily round of industry.

The day-to-day reality of keepers' lives in their towers was often a harsh one. In many cases, they had to supplement their stores. Fishing was an obvious way to do so, and many keepers took to fishing with their lines suspended from kites out over the sea. There was also gardening (if there was enough land at their station to permit this) or keeping livestock such as chickens or goats, with one poor keeper at Inishtearaght Lighthouse in Ireland falling to his death chasing after the goats to milk them. Often harsh weather could result in keepers being stranded within their tower; a serious matter if rations were running low. During the nineteenth century a ferocious, month-long storm meant that Abbie Burgess Grant, assistant keeper at the Matinicus Lighthouse, had to keep the light burning for that period in her father, the keeper's, absence. There is a famous, apocryphal tale of two marooned lighthouse keepers having to resort to eating their candles.

We tend to think of lighthouse keepers being male, which on the whole they were. America, however, has a long tradition of female keepers,

Above: Living in a lighthouse out at sea has always presented a number of logistical challenges, with even the most everyday matters taking on a challenging dimension. This photograph documents the lengths that had to be gone to in order for the keepers at Germany's Roter Sand lighthouse to receive their eight-weekly delivery of provisions, post, and newspapers.

volume than water, the great lenses could be successfully supported in a small space at the top of a tower. Furthermore, weight suspended in this way could be turned simply by the touch of a finger and so clockwork mechanisms could be used to rotate the lenses. Despite mercury's toxic nature (to which some attribute the proverbial "madness" of keepers), its advantages included the fact it was not corrosive to cast iron and also not flammable.

One of the reasons that Fresnel lenses were successfully used around the world is the fact that their modular construction meant they could be built in one place, disassembled and shipped in small, portable components then reassembled in situ. Understandably, France was the sole country of manufacture for some time. The Fresnel lenses were manufactured in six orders, with each order featuring a standard focal length (the distance from the center of the light source to the lens). These lenses such as Hannah Thomas of Gurnet Point Lighthouse, Massachusetts who manned the lighthouse from 1776–86 when her husband went off to fight the British, or Maria Younghans of Biloxi Lighthouse, Mississippi. Often women took over the post when a father or husband left it, became ill or died. Ida Lewis of Lime Rock Light Station, Rhode Island worked there during the nineteenth century, first as assistant keeper then keeper, for 39 years. During that period she saved 18 lives and following her death the House of Representatives voted to change Lime Rock's name to Ida Lewis Rock in her memory.

Working in some of the most dangerous waters known to man is naturally a hazardous job and simply reaching the lighthouse was often dangerous and challenging, with a number of keepers drowned on their way. Le Four Lighthouse, off Finistere, where waves frequently broke over the top of the tower, was so notorious that French keepers called it "Hell." Its dangerous reputation is rooted in tragic reality as in 1978 a relief boat making its way from Le Four to shore was totally swamped with a sailor and a keeper both drowned. Today, helicopters are used to maintain and relieve many lighthouses and this too is a far from risk-free procedure.

Rescuing shipwrecked mariners was also among the keeper's duties and there are many tales of great bravery. In 1838 Victorian England became entranced by the gallantry shown by Grace Darling and her father, William Darling, the keeper at Longstone Lighthouse on the Farne Islands off Northumberland's coast. Following the shipwreck of the steamer *S.S. Forfarshire* with the loss of many lives near their lighthouse, Grace and her father braved the ferocious storms in their small rowboat to rescue the nine survivors left clinging to the wreckage.

Today, of course, with the implacable march of technology, very few lighthouses around the world are still manned. In 1998 North Foreland, the last manned U.K. lighthouse became automated. Keeper Dermot Cronin, who had worked there 33 years, eloquently summed up the sadness at the loss of a human presence: "To me a lighthouse was meant to be lived in. It was part of working life. And ships passing day and night knew there was somebody there, looking at them." In France a handful of keepers remain, including those at Ile Vierge, Europe's tallest lighthouse tower. North America's only manned lighthouse is the oldest on the continent, Boston Light, established in 1716, and manned in memory of all those men and women who performed their duties as keepers. In Iceland, the remote station of Storhofoi, dramatically positioned on the austere island of Heimaey, is still manned. While the automation of lighthouses diminishes their romance, the dangers and privations that keepers had to undergo must be remembered and put into the equation.

Lighthouses continue to arouse strong loyalties and a keen following. Around the world, from Germany to America, communities are fighting to preserve their lighthouse heritage. Often lighthouses are being re-invented to allow them further life, so a German lighthouse becomes a place to conduct wedding ceremonies in its former keeper's home, American lighthouses become maritime museums or heritage centers and lighthouses as far flung as Scotland, Croatia, and California offer bed and breakfast accommodation to those who want a taste of life by the sea in these often spectacular locations.

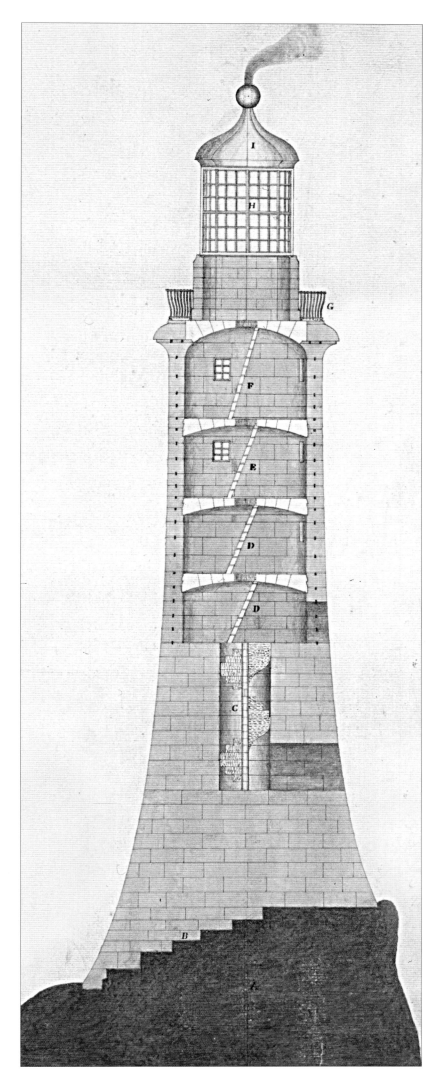

Right: A plan showing the interior layout of Smeaton's Eddystone Lighthouse.

LIGHTHOUSES OF
EUROPE

Opposite: Les Pierres Noires Lighthouse, Brittany, France: Standing firm against the formidable Atlantic waves, Les Pierres Noires, boldly banded in red and white, epitomizes the indomitable spirit of France's lighthouses. Landing here has always been perilous, so today maintenance teams are transported by helicopter, also a risky operation. Station established 1872; tower 89 ft high; status active (automated).

Above: Roches Douvres Lighthouse lantern, France: For centuries lighthouses had struggled to project their light far out enough to sea to be a significant aid to shipping. In 1822, however, the French physicist Augustin Jean Fresnel (1788–1827) made a significant breakthough, inventing the dioptric lens, whereby multiple prisms and lenses captured light and directed it into a narrow horizontal beam. Known as the Fresnel lens, this revolutionary optical apparatus was taken up by lighthouses around the world and has saved many lives at sea since its invention.

Opposite: Roches Douvres Lighthouse, Côtes d'Armor Département, France: Built from local pink granite, Roches Douvres' magnificent lighthouse warns shipping away from the dangerous reef around it. The present tower replaced a 19th-century 190-ft cast-iron tower (one of the tallest such towers ever built), prone to swaying alarmingly in strong winds, which was destroyed by the Germans during World War II. Station established 1868; present lighthouse built 1954; tower 213 ft high; status active (automated).

Above: La Vieille Lighthouse, Raz de Sein, Brittany, France: Built of granite, Brittany's "Old Lady" is one of France's most famous lighthouses. Its formidable castle-like tower acted as a prison when two of its lighthouse keepers were trapped within for three months due to severe weather.
Station established 1887; tower 89 ft high; status active (automated).

Left: Tevennec Lighthouse, France: Finistere (which means "the end of the world") is home to more lighthouses than any other region of France, among them the picturesque Feu de Tevennec, built on a small, rugged island.

Station established 1875; tower 49 ft high; status active (automated).

Opposite: Kéréon Lighthouse, Brittany, France: This striking tower, built to commemorate a young officer, Charles Marie LeDall de Kéréon, guillotined during the French Revolution, is one of France's best-known lighthouses. Its construction on the usually submerged reef on Men-Tensel off the island of Ile de Ouessant (Ushant) was a remarkable feat of engineering, which took nine years. Despite its austere exterior, the accommodation within was so sumptuous that keepers nicknamed it "the palace."
Station established 1916; tower 125 ft high; status active (automated).

Above: Belle Ile Lighthouse and hotel, Belle Ile en Mer, France: Off Brittany's coast lies the appropriately named "beautiful island." On the island, the charming port of Sauzon, with its picturesque harbor light guiding in visiting yachts and local fishermen alike, is a popular subject for photographers and painters.

Left: Island of Giraglia, Corsica: Constructed over a period of ten years, with rocks ferried across the sea and carried by donkeys to the top of the island, La Giraglia lighthouse is a legacy of the program initiated by Corsican-born Napoleon Buonaparte to build lighthouses around the French coast. Station established 1848; status active (automated).

Opposite: Port Navalo Lighthouse, France: France has a rich lighthouse heritage, ranging from dramatic granite towers which brave the Atlantic waves to picturesque harbor lights, such as this one at Port Navalo, Arzon, Brittany. The French term for small lights or harbor lights is "feu" (meaning fire), with the term "phare" reserved for large, coastal lighthouses. These smaller beacons act as guiding lights, leading boats into harbor.

Above: Pointe des Poulains, Belle Ile, France: Situated on an islet off the coast of Belle Ile, Le Phare des Poulains has been active since 1868.

Opposite: La Coubre Lighthouse, France: The top third of La Coubre's tall, slender tower is painted a striking red, with the remaining two-thirds painted white. The current tower, which replaced two lighthouses endangered by soil erosion, was built one mile from the sea but today, because of continuing erosion, the shore is within 800 ft of the lighthouse.
Station established 1830; present lighthouse built 1905; tower 213 ft high; status active (automated).

Above: La Jument Lighthouse, Brittany, France: Erected on a rock often submerged beneath the waves, work on La Jument tower progressed slowly, taking nine years to complete. Its construction in the first place was thanks to the generosity of M. Charles Paton, who bequeathed a considerable sum to have a new lighthouse built in the Ouessant region.
Station established 1911; tower 157 ft high; status active (automated).

Left: Ile Vierge, off the Brittany coast, France: The small island of Ile Vierge houses two contrasting lighthouses. The first lighthouse, a square white tower built on top of the keeper's dwelling, was deactivated in 1902 (though it still houses the station's fog signal) and is now known as "le petit phare" (the little lighthouse) as it stands dwarfed by its neighbor, Europe's tallest lighthouse and the tallest stone lighthouse ever built, a slender, graceful tower constructed in 1902 whose light can be seen for an impressive 31 miles.

Station established 1845; present lighthouse built 1902; 1845 tower 102 ft high; 1902 tower 270 ft high; status active (manned).

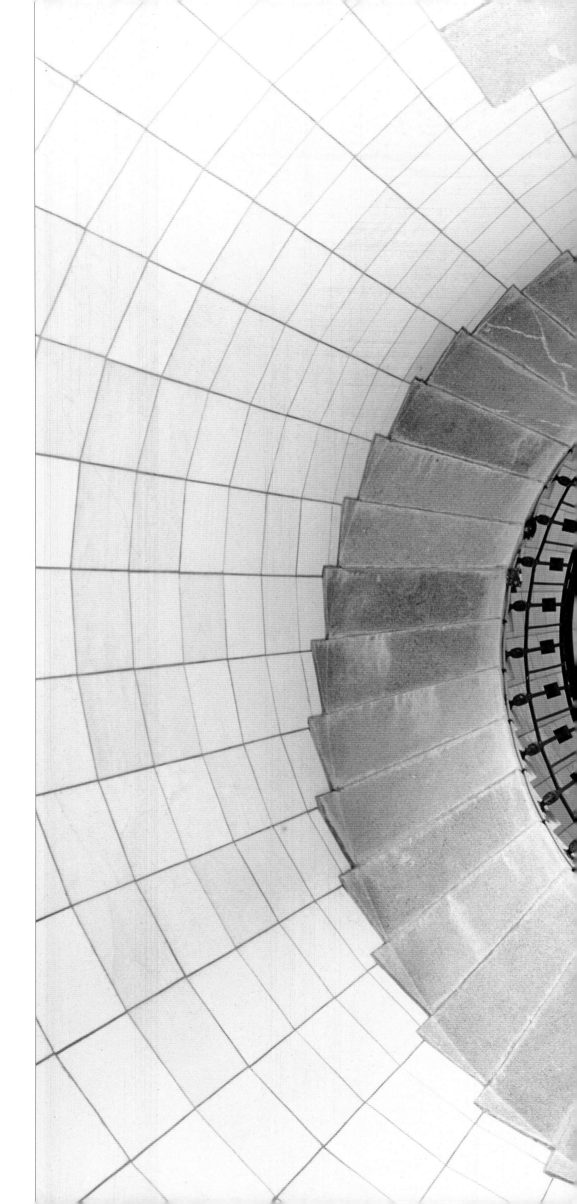

Right: Staircase at Ile Vierge, France: This exquisite staircase, resembling a nautilus shell, spirals up inside Ile Vierge lighthouse, which at 270 ft high is Europe's tallest. One of France's last manned lighthouses, the keeper here has a 397-step climb to reach the control room.
Station established 1845; present lighthouse built 1902; status active (manned).

Opposite: Cordouan Lighthouse, Gironde, France: France's oldest lighthouse, at the mouth of the Gironde River, is a unique, graceful structure, built on the site of an ancient beacon. It was commissioned by Henry III from the architect Louis de Foix in 1584 and finished in 1610. Built in lavish style, complete with royal apartments and a chapel, Cordouan Lighthouse, alongside Notre-Dame de Paris, was one of the first two buildings to be classified as a "monument historique". It was at this historic lighthouse that Augustin Jean Fresnel tested his revolutionary new optical system and in 1823 Cordouan became the first lighthouse in the world to have the Fresnel lens installed.

Present lighthouse built 1584–1610; tower 223 ft high; status active (manned).

Right: Pointe de St Mathieu Lighthouse, Brittany, France: This slender tower, constructed in the 19th century, was built among the ruins of a Benedictine abbey. The tradition of a warning light on this headland dates back to 1692 when the monks began showing a light from the abbey tower.

Station established 1692; present lighthouse built 1835; tower 121 ft high; status active (automated).

Left: Beachy Head and Seven Sisters chalk cliffs, England: Beachy Head Lighthouse — an indomitable lighthouse at the edge of the sea dwarfed by the great white cliffs towering behind it — forms a quintessential image of the English coastline. In fact, the first lighthouse at Beachy Head, Belle Tout, was situated on top of the cliffs (where severe erosion resulted in it being moved back away from the crumbling cliff edge in 1999), but it was superseded by the current lighthouse in 1902.

Station established 1828; present lighthouse built 1902; tower 142 ft high; status active (automated).

Opposite: Beachy Head, the Isle of Wight, England: Jauntily striped in red and white, this iconic lighthouse was built in 1902. Its construction at the base of the cliffs was a considerable feat, involving building a coffer-dam to surround the site and a cableway to carry material down from the top of the cliffs, with an impressive 3660 tons of Cornish granite used in its construction.

Station established 1828; present lighthouse built 1902; tower 142 ft high; status active (automated).

Above: Jutting out into the sea off the western side of the Isle of Wight, the Needles rocks were an infamous hazard to shipping en route to Portsmouth and Southampton. In response to pleas from local shipmasters, Trinity House (the organization overseeing lighthouse construction in Britain) built a lighthouse on the cliffs above the rocks in 1786. Too often obscured by fog, however, this proved ineffectual. Finally, in 1858, the present lighthouse was built, this time on the furthest chalk stack or "Needle," with the foundations dug deep out of the rock.

Station established 1786; present tower built 1858; tower 72 ft high; status active (automated).

Right: Neist Point Lighthouse, Isle of Skye, Scotland: Perched dramatically on the cliffs at the northeast corner of the lovely Isle of Skye, Neist Point Lighthouse was built to guide shipping through the channel between Skye and the Outer Hebrides. Today, with the lighthouse automated, the keepers' cottages have been converted into holiday accommodation, offering visitors the opportunity to experience life in this beautiful, remote setting.

Station established 1909; tower 62 ft high; status active (automated).

Opposite: Trevose Head Lighthouse, Cornwall, England: A much-needed marker on the treacherous north Cornish coast where sailors faced dense fogs and sea mist, Trevose Head originally had two white lights (one high and one low), a way for mariners to identify it. During the 19th century, rotating the light became the favored way of providing distinctive light patterns.

Station established 1847; tower 87 ft high; status active (automated).

Above: Rubha Reidh Lighthouse, Scotland: Looking out across the great sea channel known as The Minch, this neat, white lighthouse has witnessed many formidable storms. During World War II, two of the keepers here played a considerable part in rescuing survivors from the American liberty ship *William H. Welch*, which had missed its way and come ashore during a severe gale.

Station established 1912; tower 82 ft high; status active (automated).

Previous pages: Godrevy, Cornwall, England: Cornwall's many visitors today come to enjoy the sea and many forget how historically dangerous the Cornish coast was to shipping. Constructed to warn sailors of The Stones, a dangerous one-and-a-half-mile long reef off St. Ives, the final impetus to build Godrevy Lighthouse came with the wrecking of *The Nile* on The Stones in 1854, with all lives on board tragically lost. Five years later the lighthouse was completed and it warns of The Stones to this day.

Station established 1859; tower 86 ft high; status active (automated).

Opposite: Barra Head Lighthouse, Western Isles, Scotland: Scotland's notoriously treacherous coastline offered considerable challenges to lighthouse builders. One man who successfully overcame these challenges was the noted engineer Robert Stevenson (1772–1850) whose Barra Head Lighthouse, built in 1833, still warns shipping to this day. Stevenson was followed in his profession by his sons and grandsons, with the Stevenson dynasty building 97 lighthouses in all. The black sheep of the family was his grandson Robert Louis Stevenson, who chose to write books instead of building lighthouses and is remembered today as the author of *Treasure Island.*

Station established 1833; tower 60 ft high; status active (automated).

Left: Inishtearaght, County Kerry, Ireland: Dramatically situated on the austere slopes of one of the Blasket Islands off Ireland's west coast, this is famed as Europe's most westerly lighthouse (Iceland excepted). Constructing it took six grueling years of blasting rock and building. Living here was always challenging, with, in 1913, one poor assistant keeper falling to his death while trying to catch the goats for milking.

Station established 1870; tower 56 ft high; status active (automated).

Left: Fastnet Lighthouse, off the south coast of Ireland: Known as "the teardrop of Ireland," Fastnet Lighthouse was the last sight of Ireland for the thousands of Irish emigrants sailing to America. The first lighthouse on this remote spot was built in 1854 against formidable odds, but so battered by the elements (including a gale in 1881 which broke the glass in the lantern) that it was replaced at the turn of the 20th century with a stronger structure consisting of dovetailed Cornish granite, built in sections in Cornwall and shipped over on a purpose-built vessel.

Station established 1854; present lighthouse 1903; tower 177 ft high; status active (automated).

Opposite: Old Head of Kinsale, County Cork, Ireland: Today's striking black and white lighthouse is the third to be built on the Old Head to guide ships into Kinsale Harbor. The first lighthouse here was built in 1665, with the light provided by an open coal fire on its roof.
Station established 1665; present lighthouse built 1853; tower 100 ft high; status active.

Above: Longstone Lighthouse, Farne Islands, Northumberland, England: This solid-looking Northumbrian lighthouse witnessed a heroic deed which became the stuff of legends in Victorian Britain. The dangerous rocks nearby claimed the *S.S. Forfarshire* in 1838, with the loss of many lives though nine survivors clung on to the ship's wreck. Longstone lighthouse keeper William Darling, together with his daughter Grace, twice braved the still formidable seas in a small, open rowboat to rescue the wreck's survivors. So dreadful was the storm that they had to wait two days in the lighthouse until it had abated and the survivors could finally be taken to the mainland. Grace Darling's courage caught the nation's imagination and she was feted as a heroine.
Station established 1826; tower 86 ft high; status active (automated).

Left: Skellig Michael Lighthouse, Ireland: During the 19th century, engineer George Halpin Senior played a major part in constructing and designing Ireland's lighthouses. Among them were the original upper and lower lighthouse towers on Skellig Michael, a rocky island which had been home to a monastic community since the 7th century.

Station established 1826; Skellig Michael high built 1826; tower 24 ft high; status inactive since 1870; Skellig Michael low built 1967; tower 31 ft high; status active (automated).

Opposite: Poolbeg Light, Dublin Bay, Ireland: At the end of one of Europe's longest sea walls, extending from Ringsend nearly four miles out into Dublin Bay, sits Poolbeg Light, nowadays painted a cheery red.
Station established 1768; present light built 1820; tower 66 ft high; status active (automated).

Right: Wolf Rock, Cornwall, England: Off Land's End, on an outcrop named evocatively after the howl of the wind in the fissures of the rock, it's hard to imagine a bleaker spot in which to construct a lighthouse. Ever since 1795, when a daymark had been placed on the rock, men had struggled to build a lasting beacon. Work on a granite tower began in 1861 but, due to adverse conditions, was not completed until 1869.

 Shipwrecks, though disastrous for the crew and the ship owners, were often profitable for the local seashore communities. Cargo was divided into four categories: "flotsam" was cargo that floated, "jetsam" was cargo that had been jettisoned, "ligan" was cargo that sank and was marked with a buoy, and "wreck" was the cargo that washed ashore. So dangerous was Wolf Rock, and hence so profitable to wreckers, that before the construction of the present lighthouse, local wreckers blocked the cavern in case the sound of the howl alerted shipping to the rock's presence.
Station established 1795; present tower built 1869; tower 134 ft high; status active (automated).

Right: Howth Pier, County Dublin, Ireland: A reassuring sight, this small, solid stone-built harbor light built on the end of Howth Pier guided shipping into the harbor for over 160 years until its role was taken over by a modern tower constructed nearby.
Station established 1818; tower 33 ft high; status deactivated 1982.

Opposite: Roter Sand Lighthouse, Germany: Despite this peaceful image, Roter Sand, one of Germany's most famous lighthouses, has borne the brunt of high seas and huge waves standing as it does in the North Sea. Its construction out at sea was a considerable engineering feat since it was the first fixed light to be built in the open sea on quicksand by using a caisson. A caisson is a large open-ended cylinder which is positioned on the seabed then sunk to the bedrock. As the caisson is lowered to the bedrock, it is extended by adding extra sections so that the top remains above high water level. Once in place, the caisson is pumped dry and filled with concrete in order to provide a base for a lighthouse. The first attempt along these lines at Roter Sand met with disaster when, in 1881, the incomplete caisson broke and sank in a violent hurricane. In 1883, however, a second caisson was successfully placed on the bottom of the sea with the lighthouse finally operational in 1885. Although no longer in use, it is open for tours and overnight stays.
Station established 1885; tower 92 ft high; status inactive since 1986.

Above: Westerheversand Lighthouse, Schleswig-Holstein, Germany: Flanked by keeper's cottages on either side, Westheversand is today a popular site for weddings, with one of the cottages now licensed to conduct wedding ceremonies.
Station established 1908; tower 131 ft high; status active.

Right: Lindau, Lake Constance, Bavaria Germany: This graceful tower on Lake Constance is a historic landmark, still in use today guiding the yachts and sailboats into the busy harbor at Lindau.

Station established 1856; tower 108 ft high; status active (automated).

Opposite: Darsser Ort Lighthouse, Mecklenburg, Germany: One of the oldest lighthouses on the Baltic Sea coast, Darsser Ort is today a popular and much-visited lighthouse with visitors enjoying not only spectacular views over the Baltic from the tower but also a nature museum in the lighthouse buildings.
Station established 1848; tower 115 ft high; status active (automated).

Above: Bremerhaven Lighthouse, Germany: Strikingly decorative, this New Gothic structure evokes a church or a castle tower but is, in fact, one of the many working lighthouses in the busy German port of Bremerhaven.
Station established 1855; tower 121 ft high; status active (automated).

Opposite: Lange Jaap (Long John) Lighthouse, Den Helder, Holland: A country with a long and notable maritime tradition, the Netherlands is home to a large number of historic lighthouses. Today these are lovingly preserved by a nation keen to protect its lighthouse tradition. Among them is Long John, a classically elegant construction by Dutch lighthouse engineer Quirinius Harder, built in 1878. The cast-iron, 16-sided tower competes for the title of the world's tallest cast-iron lighthouse with New Caledonia's Phare Amedee, far away on the other side of the world.
Station established 1882; present light built 1878; tower 180 ft high; status active (automated).

Above: List Ost on Sylt, Schleswig-Holstein, Germany: A popular landmark among the sand dunes on the island of Sylt, this was built by the Danish government during the 19th century to guide ships along the channel between Sylt and the Danish island of Romo. Although currently still active, the future of this and many other historic German lighthouses as functioning navigational aids is in question.
Station established 1858; tower 43 ft high; status active (automated).

Opposite: Aero Island, Denmark: With a seafaring tradition going back to the Vikings, Denmark also has a venerable tradition of constructing lighthouses, with the Royal Danish Lighthouse Authority founded in 1560. Today the Royal Danish Administration of Navigation and Hydrography operates 195 lighthouses in Denmark, including this one on Aero Island.

Above: Isla de Vearoy, Lofoten Islands, Norway: The archipelago is famous for its cod and stockfish. With 80 percent of the population on the island of Vaeroy earning their living from fishing, this small, homely looking lighthouse has an important role within the community.

Opposite: Kvitholmen Lighthouse, near Kristiansund, Norway: On this small rocky island, Kvitholmen lighthouse (with its old and new towers in close proximity) warns shipping of the imminent dangers of the Hustadvika waters, considered one of the most dangerous stretches along the Norwegian coast.
Station established 1842; old tower 36 ft high; status active (automated).

Above: Kjeungskjaer Lighthouse, near Trondheim, Norway: This intriguing red lighthouse in the middle of the water near the historic city of Trondheim and the picturesque village of Rorvik, is a popular sight for tourists enjoying a boat journey around Norway's coast.
Station established 1880; status active (automated).

Right: Krossnes Lighthouse, Iceland: Painted a bright orange for maximum visibility against the surrounding snowy white landscape, Krossnes, with its squat, square tower, is an archetypal Icelandic lighthouse.

Station established 1926; tower 29 ft high; status active (automated).

Opposite: Thridrangi Lighthouse, Iceland: Smartly painted in red and white, Thridrangi Lighthouse somehow manages to look homely and reassuring, despite its isolated position on a formidable, sharp lava outcrop jutting out of the North Atlantic waters. Due to its remote location the station was never manned.
Station established 1942; tower 13 ft high; status active (automated).

Above: Sugandisey, Iceland: This diminutive lighthouse squats on tall cliffs over the entrance of the harbor of Stykkisholmur. It is an ingenious example of recycling, consisting as it does of the lantern of the older Grotta lighthouse, built in 1897.
Station established 1948; tower 11 ft high; status active (automated).

Right: Storhofoi Lighthouse, Vestmannaeyjar, Iceland: Strikingly isolated on this remote volcanic island, the Storhofoi lighthouse is the highest in Iceland, standing around 410 ft above sea level, and is one of the few Icelandic lighthouses still manned by keepers.

Station established 1906; tower 23 ft high; status active (manned).

Opposite: Punta Cavazzi Lighthouse, Ustica Island, Sicily: The Italians possess a venerable tradition of lighthouse construction, dating back to the Romans. This lighthouse today stands guard over a popular snorkeling spot off the Sicilian island of Ustica, designated a marine reserve.

Above: Light at entrance to Venice's lagoon: The beautiful city of Venice achieved glory through its status as a formidable maritime power and center of trade. Reaching Venice by boat remains, to this day, a memorable experience, but care is needed to find one's way through the many channels across the great lagoon, with this light one of many set in place to guide mariners.

Left: El Rompido Lighthouse, Huelva, Spain: Because of the curvature of the earth, lighthouses have been either tall or built high up in order to maximize the distance at which their light can be seen. This 19th-century lighthouse at El Rompido has been superseded by its much younger and taller substitute, looming over it in the background.

Station established 1861; present lighthouse built 1975; tower 95 ft high; status active.

Opposite: An 18th-century stone-built lighthouse in the province of Murcia, Spain. The power of the light in a modern lighthouse is measured in candelas, one candela being roughly equivalent to one two-hundredth of a 50-watt bulb, with some lamps being capable of emitting one million candelas. However, at the beginning of the 18th century, light was still being generated by bonfires burning wood or coal.

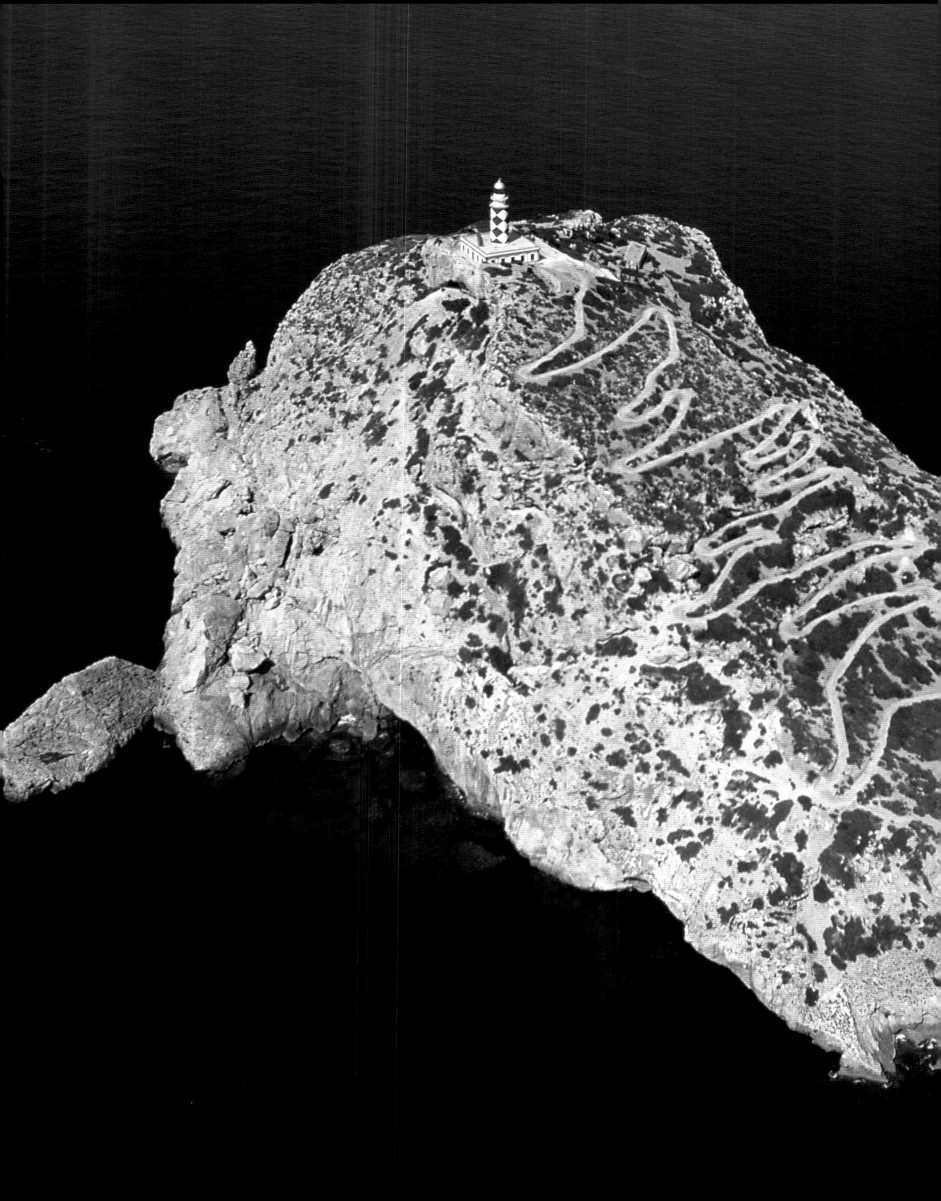

Left: The Cabrera archipelago, south of the island of Majorca, has a rich maritime history; used by the Phoenicians, Greeks, and Romans on their trading routes, it was also a historic haven for pirates. Today, more peacefully, the archipelago is a national park, with its lighthouse watching over the bird colonies for which Cabrera is famous.

Opposite: Trafalgar Lighthouse, Trafalgar Bay, Spain: This imposing lighthouse on Cape Trafalgar looks out over the scene of the Battle of Trafalgar in 1805, the pivotal sea battle in the Napoleonic Wars when the English fleet defeated the combined French and Spanish fleet. The evocatively named "Playa de las Almas" ("beach of souls") in the bay below was named in memory of the bodies washed up after the battle.

Above: Chipiona, Cadiz, Spain: The ancient sea ports of Cadiz were developed by the Phoenicians, Greeks, and Romans, with an old lighthouse, modeled on the Pharos of Alexandria, constructed by the Romans at the mouth of the River Guadalquivir. Today, the picturesque town of Chipiona is dominated by Spain's tallest lighthouse, a magnificent 19th-century edifice.
Station established in Roman times; present lighthouse built 1867; tower 206 ft high.

Previous pages: Belem Tower, Lisbon: A majestic sight in Lisbon Harbor, the Tower of Belem was built in 1515 to defend the River Tagus and is a monument to Portugal's great Age of Discovery, when Portuguese explorers and navigators laid the foundations for European maritime domination. Over the centuries, this impressive monument has served as a telegraph station, a customs checkpoint, a prison and a lighthouse. Today it is a UNESCO World Heritage Site.

Opposite: Lighthouse on the Cape of St. Vincent, Algarve, Portugal: The lighthouse at Cabo de Sao Vicente (a landmark cape jutting out into the Atlantic which was the site for a number of major sea battles) has a venerable history, with its origins in a beacon lit by monks in 1515 at a monastery on this spot.
Station established 1846; tower 88 ft high; status active (automated).

Above: Agiogi Theodori, Argostoli, Cephalonia: This charming Cephalonian lighthouse, whimsically built in the shape of a Greek temple, was originally constructed in 1818 but had to be rebuilt after the 1953 earthquake.
Station established 1818; present tower built 1953; tower 26 ft high; status active (automated).

Above: Rhodes Lighthouse, Greece: In ancient history, the 110 ft-high Colossus of Rhodes, one of the Seven Wonders of the World, that loomed over the harbor is said to have been used as a beacon guiding mariners. Today's Mandraki Harbor features the Fortress of St. Nicholas, with its 1863 harbor lighthouse, constructed on a far smaller scale.
Present station built 1863; tower 20 ft high.

Opposite: Firkas Tower at Chania Harbor, Greece: with its myriad islands and rich maritime heritage, Greece boasts a number of historic lighthouses. Chania's first lighthouse was constructed over 500 years ago, with today's elegant, minaret-like tower built in the 19th century during a period of Egyptian occupation.
Present station built 1840; status deactivated.

Right: Pokonji Dol Island, Croatia: Many of Croatia's lighthouses are today being promoted as tourist accommodation in peaceful natural surroundings. Close to the historic town of Hvar, this picturesque lighthouse on the tiny island of Pokonji Dol is a popular spot for kayakers and snorkelers.

LIGHTHOUSES OF
NORTH AMERICA

Opposite: Sakonet Lighthouse, Rhode Island: Construction began near Little Compton in 1883, when an iron pier was placed by Little Cormorant Rock and filled with concrete. Heavy winter seas caused delays, but work was completed in 1884. Rowing to and from the lighthouse was very dangerous, with assistant keeper Walter Smiley swept out of his boat in 1911; he was rescued by an elderly couple who were on the shore.

Above: Marshall Point Lighthouse, Maine: During the 19th century Port Clyde became a busy port, home to fish canneries, quarries, and shipbuilders. The first lighthouse was erected in 1832 at Marshall Point to help mariners entering Port Clyde Harbor. This was a 20-ft high rubblestone tower, lit by seven lard oil lamps with 14-inch reflectors. The present lighthouse, which replaced it, was built in 1857 and featured a fixed white light visible for 10 miles. In 1878 a bell tower with 1000-lb bronze bell was built at the station. This impressive bell was replaced by a horn in 1969. The walkway in the photograph connected the lighthouse to the keeper's house and was originally covered.

Station established 1832; present lighthouse 1857; tower 31 ft high; status active (automated).

Right: Castle Hill Lighthouse, Rhode Island: This peaceful scene belies the difficulties experienced in constructing the lighthouse, not because of the elements but because of powerful local opposition. In 1874 Congress authorized $10,000 for the creation of a fog signal on Castle Hill at Narragansett Bay, to help mariners through the East Passage. Harvard professor Alexander Agassiz had a summer cottage on Castle Hill and opposed the plan, refusing to sell any of his land as he objected to the idea of a loud fog bell. In 1886 it was proposed a lighthouse be constructed too. Agassiz finally sold a bit of land to the government but initially refused to grant the right of way, which meant the bringing of materials by sea. The lighthouse was completed in 1890 and a fog bell was operational for one and a half years, though discontinued when Agassiz objected. Five years later, the original bell was replaced with a louder one, to which Agassiz objected too.

Station established 1890; tower 34 ft high; original optic fifth order Fresnel; present optic 300 mm; status active (automated).

Opposite: Sandy Hook Lighthouse, New Jersey: The oldest continuously operating lighthouse in the United States, Sandy Hook was designed and built by Isaac Contro in 1764, becoming the fifth lighthouse to be built in North America. It is a striking stone, octagonal, nine-story tower, 85 ft high. Surviving attempts by the British to disrupt its service and damage it during the Revolutionary War the lighthouse continued to shine out through the following centuries and became the first American lighthouse to be lit by electric incandescent lamps. Originally the lighthouse stood around 500 ft from the tip of the Hook; today, due to the expansion of the Hook, it stands 1.5 miles from the point.

Station established 1764; tower 85 ft high; original optic 18 lamps with 21 refractors; present optic third order Fresnel; status active (automated).

Above: New London Ledge Lighthouse, Connecticut: This is a unique building, one of the last lighthouses to be constructed in New England and a rare case of an early 20th-century offshore lighthouse not constructed from cast iron. The New London Ledge Lighthouse was built in the French Second Empire style to satisfy the wealthy local homeowners who wanted a lighthouse in keeping with their elegant residences. Despite its attractive appearance, the lighthouse is rumored to be haunted by a ghost called "Ernie," a keeper who jumped to his death from the lighthouse roof when he learned that his wife had run off with the captain of the Block Island Ferry.

Station established 1909; tower 58 ft high; original optic fourth order Fresnel; present optic 190 mm; status active (automated).

Previous pages: Pond Island Lighthouse, Maine: This small tower marks the mouth of the Kennebec River. During the 1820s Pond Island became a transfer point for steamer passengers traveling from Augusta to Bangor and a stone lighthouse was erected in 1821. This was replaced by the present lighthouse in 1855. Today the small, treeless island is managed as a nature reserve with the lighthouse still used as an active aid to navigation.

Station established 1821; present lighthouse built 1855; tower 20 ft high; original optic fifth order Fresnel; present optic 250 mm; status active (automated).

Left: Block Island Southeast Light, Rhode Island: This striking-looking lighthouse, a 52-ft octagonal tower capped with a 16-sided cast-iron lantern, is the highest light in New England. The building with its attached lighthouse keeper's house is a fascinating medley of the Italianate and Gothic Revival styles popular at the time of its construction in 1875. Block Island, on which it stands, is so surrounded by dangerous ledges and shoals that it was known as the "stumbling block" of the New England coast. With dozens of vessels sunk along this part of the coast, the Lighthouse Service decided to construct two lighthouses: the North Light in 1829 followed by the Southeast Light in 1875.

Over the decades, soil erosion meant that the structure, originally 300 ft from the edge of the bluff, found itself only 55 ft from the brink. Remarkably, the entire structure was successfully moved back 300 ft from the edge.

Station established 1875; deactivated 1990; relit 1994; tower 52 ft high; original optic first order Fresnel; present optic also a first order Fresnel.

Opposite: Cape Neddick Lighthouse, Maine: Built on the Nubble (a small, rocky island off the eastern point of Cape Neddick), the light was built in 1879 to mark the entrance to the York River. Mariners had been asking for a lighthouse since 1807 and indeed the ghost ship of the *Isidore,* wrecked in 1824 north of the Nubble, is rumored to haunt the local waters. The lighthouse keepers at the Nubble rowed to and from the island and also used a bucket suspended on a line across the channel to transport supplies. In fact, in 1967, the keeper put his child in the bucket and sent him on his way to school each day!
Station established 1879; tower 41 ft high; status active (automated).

Left: Sankaty Head Light, Siasconset, Massachusetts: A much-loved legacy of Nantucket's whaling heritage, Sankaty Light was constructed in 1850 to help guide busy shipping traffic. It was the first lighthouse in the U.S. to have a Fresnel lens as part of its original equipment. So powerful was the light cast by this lens that it could apparently be seen 40 miles away and was known by local sailors as "the blazing star."
Station established 1850; tower 70 ft high; original optic second order Fresnel; present optic DCB 224; status active.

Left: West Quoddy Light, Maine: This striking candy-striped lighthouse, positioned on the easternmost part of the United States mainland, is a frequently depicted, iconic American lighthouse. Although Canadian lighthouses are frequently red-striped, to help them stand out against the snowy landscape, stripes are rarely seen in the United States although Assateague Light in Virginia is one of the most famous examples.

Station established 1808; present lighthouse 1858; tower 49 ft high; original optic third order Fresnel, 1858 (still in use).

Opposite: As lighting systems developed in complexity, the use of colored glass and flashing lights enabled lighthouses to have differing, identifying signals from each other, so providing sailors with a key navigational aid.

Above: East Point Lighthouse, New Jersey: The tranquility of this scene belies the lighthouse's checkered history. Built in 1849 at the mouth of the Maurice River it had helped commercial oyster fishers navigate through the Delaware Bay for almost 100 years when it was decommissioned. Having fallen into disrepair, a legal dispute over ownership saw further decline followed, in 1971, by an act of arson. Thanks to the efforts of the Maurice River Historical Society, however, it was restored and relit in 1980 and is still in use today.

Station established 1852; tower 40 ft high; original optic sixth order Fresnel; present 250 mm; status active (automated 1911; decommissioned in 1941; restored and relit 1980).

Right: Bass Harbor Head Lighthouse, Maine: Built in the most scenic of spots, on Mount Desert Island, this small, demure, white lighthouse was constructed in 1858 to warn mariners of the Bass Harbor bar at the eastern entrance to the harbor. A fog bell and a bell tower were added in 1876 and replaced in 1898. Today the lighthouse, although not open to the public, forms a popular tourist attraction.

Station established 1858; tower 32 ft high; original optic fifth order Fresnel; present optic: fourth order Fresnel (1902); status active (automated).

Following pages: Portland Head Lighthouse, Portland, Maine: This spectacular New England lighthouse was built in 1791 on Cape Elizabeth to mark the entrance to Portland Harbor, then a busy port. President George Washington appointed Captain Joseph Greenleaf, a Revolutionary War veteran, to be its first keeper.

The lighthouse was well known by the famous American poet Henry Wadsworth Longfellow as a young man and inspired his poem "The Lighthouse":

> "The rocky ledge runs far into the sea
> And on its outer point, some miles away,
> The lighthouse lifts its massive masonry
> A pillar of fire by night, of cloud by day."

Station established 1791; tower 80 ft high; original optic fourth order Fresnel; present optic DCB 224.

Opposite: Montauk Point Lighthouse, Long Island, New York: New York State's oldest lighthouse, with its bold 110-ft tower, still operates proudly to this very day. Authorized by the Second Congress under President George Washington in 1792, construction, which began in June 1796, was speedily completed by November 5 of the same year. Due to its position on the east end of Long Island, this was the first visible symbol of the New World to greet the millions of immigrants coming into New York Harbor.
Station established 1796; light first lit 1797; tower 110 ft high; original optic 13 whale oil lamps; present optic DCB-224 (1987); status active (automated).

Above: Sandy Point Shoal Light, Skidmore, Maryland: This striking, octagonal Empire-style lighthouse in Chesapeake Bay, still an active aid to navigation, consists of a brick tower resting on wooden caisson foundations, a fine example of the engineering involved in building structures in deep water.
Station established 1883; tower 37 ft high; original optic fourth order Fresnel; present optic 300 mm solar-powered; active (automated).

Right: Stage Harbor Lighthouse, Chatham, Cape Cod, Massachusetts: There is a rather melancholy air about this Cape Cod lighthouse, built in 1880 to guide vessels into Old Stage Harbor. In 1918 its keeper, a man called Gunderson, committed suicide and in 1933 the lighthouse was deactivated, replaced by an automated light on a skeleton tower.

Opposite: Portsmouth Lighthouse, Fort Constitution, New Castle, New Hampshire: Marking the mouth of the Piscataya River, the present lighthouse dates back to 1878, although the station was originally established in 1771 with a 50-ft-high wooden lighthouse. Solidly constructed of cast iron, it is a classic example of the hard-wearing, low-maintenance lighthouses developed by America's Lighthouse Board.

Above: The Bug Light, Long Beach Bar, Long Island: Affectionately nicknamed "the bug light" due to its resemblance to a water beetle, thanks to its screw-pile "legs," today's structure is a replica of the 19th-century original, sadly destroyed by arson in 1963. In 1911 the steamer *Shinnecock* ran aground in thick fog close to the lighthouse, due to negligence by the then keeper, who had failed to sound the fog bell in time. Fortunately no-one was drowned in the incident but it was a telling demonstration of the constant, dutiful vigilance required of lighthouse keepers.

Station established 1871; discontinued 1948; destroyed by fire 1963; rebuilt and relit 1990; original optic fifth order Fresnel; present optic 250 mm; status active (automated).

Left: Grand Haven South Pier Lights, Lake Michigan: These wonderfully atmospheric lights, positioned at the end of a pier which stretches out 1100 ft into Lake Michigan, form part of a chain of lighthouses built to guide shipping along the lake's coast. The two tower lights, each positioned at different heights, were designed to be lined up by ships one above the other, so that they could approach the harbor in a straight line.

Station established 1839; present lights 1905; outer tower 36 ft high, inner tower 51 ft high; original optic sixth order Fresnel; present optic 250 mm outer, 190 mm inner; status active (automated).

Following pages: Split Rock Lighthouse, Lake Superior, Minnesota: Dramatically positioned on a craggy cliff overlooking Lake Superior, the Split Rock Lighthouse, built to aid the iron ore shipping trade, is a tribute to the tenacity and skill of the men who constructed it. The man in charge of the project, Ralph Russell Tinkhorn, went on to become the Chief Engineer of the U.S. Lighthouse Service.

Station established 1910; tower 54 ft high; original optic third order Fresnel; status deactivated (1969).

Above: Grosse Point, Illinois: The historic lighthouse at Grosse Point owes its origins to Chicago's industrial growth during the 1870s. So much smoke was produced by the city's industries that navigating Lake Michigan had become a hazardous affair. Engineer Orlando M. Poe was put in charge of building the tower at Grosse Point, a major promontory 13 miles north of Chicago Harbor. Constructed out of cream city brick, the splendid tower is an archetypal Great Lakes lighthouse station, today housing a maritime museum.

Station established 1873; tower 113 ft high; status inactive 1941–46, reactivated and privately maintained (automated).

Above: Grand Island East Channel Lighthouse, Michigan: This combined wooden dwelling and tower, characteristic of the Great Lake lighthouses, was once painted white to act as a landmark. Plagued by maintenance problems because of its position close to the water's edge, it was deactivated in 1908 and is today a neglected shadow of its former self.

Station established 1868; tower 45 ft high; status deactivated.

Opposite: Old Mackinac Point Lighthouse, Mackinaw City, Michigan: This splendid castle-like construction was built, after much delay, to help vessels through the foggy Straits of Mackinac. The opening of the illuminated Mackinac Bridge in 1957, putting the car ferries that had depended on the light out of business, saw the lighthouse deactivated in the same year, though fortunately preserved as a museum.

Station established 1890; light first lit in 1892; tower 40 ft high; original optic fourth order Fresnel; status inactive.

Above: Holland Harbor Lighthouse, Holland, Michigan: With its gabled roofs reflecting the Dutch influence in the area, this local landmark is affectionately known as "Big Red," for obvious reasons. This bright scarlet color allowed it to conform to the "Red Right Return" standard, which called for all aids to navigation located on the right side of a harbor entrance to be red.

Station established 1870; tower 32 ft high; original optic fourth order Fresnel; present optic 250 mm; status active (automated).

Left: Cape Hatteras, North Carolina: America's tallest lighthouse tower, an impressive 193 ft high, has watched over the infamous Diamond Straits since 1870. Severe coastal erosion, however, meant that the tower, initially built 1600 ft from the sea, was by 1987 only 120 ft inland. In 1999, therefore, in an impressive feat of engineering, construction, and conservation skills, the tower was successfully rolled half a mile inland, a tribute to the national affection in which this landmark tower is held.

Station established 1797; present tower built 1870; tower 193 ft high; original optic first order Fresnel; current optic DCB-24.

Following pages: Biloxi Lighthouse, Mississippi: America's second-oldest cast-iron lighthouse stands today rather incongruously in the center of Highway 90. Among its claims to fame is the number of female lighthouse keepers who have operated it: Mary Reynolds (keeper 1854–66), then Maria Younghans for a remarkable 51 years (keeper 1867–1918), then her daughter Miranda Younghans (keeper 1919–29).

Station established 1848; tower 61 ft high; original optic fifth order Fresnel; present optic fourth order Fresnel (1926); status active (automated).

Opposite: Key West Lighthouse, Florida: This attractive lighthouse, nowadays a museum, is a reminder of the historic importance of Key West as an outpost for trade between the Atlantic and the Gulf of Mexico. Although the present tower has survived much severe battering, its predecessor collapsed in an 1846 hurricane.

Station established 1826; present tower 1848; original optic 3 Argand lamps with 21-inch reflectors; status inactive.

Above: Sombrero Lighthouse, Sombrero Coral Reef, Marathon, Florida: Towering above the coral reef, this distinctive-looking construction, a screw-pile, skeletal tower made from wrought iron and wood, is the tallest of the unique Florida Keys Reef Lights, the largest collection of iron-pile lighthouses in the world.

Station established 1858; tower 156 ft high; original optic first order Fresnel; present optic VRB-25 rotating beacon.

Left: Cape Florida Lighthouse, Key Biscayne, Florida: This peaceful scene belies the lighthouse's turbulent history. A ferocious attack by Seminole Indians resulted in the first tower at this station being extinguished between 1836–46. The current tower, built in 1846, was attacked in 1861 during the Civil War and not relit until 1867. Despite these vicissitudes, the tower is still operational to this day.

Station established 1825; present tower 1846; original optic 17 Argand lamps with 21-inch reflectors; present optic 300 mm; status active (automated).

Opposite: Tybee Island Lighthouse, Tybee Island, Georgia: Dramatically painted in black and white bands, the Tybee Island lighthouse marks the entrance to the Savannah River. The original lighthouse, built in 1736, stood a magnificent 90 ft tall, making it the tallest structure of its kind in America at that time, but was swept away in a storm in 1741. A replacement tower, built in 1773, was largely destroyed by Confederate troops during the Civil War to prevent Federal troops using it. Today's lighthouse, built in 1867, uses the lower 60 ft of that 1773 tower as its foundation.

Station established 1736; present light 1867; tower 145 ft high; original optic oil lamps: present optic first order Fresnel; status active (automated).

Left: Port Wilson Lighthouse, Washington: This classic lighthouse stands at a point where the main shipping channel narrows and turns into Puget Sound. Captain J. W. Sheldon donated a ship's bell to the town's St. Paul's Episcopal Church in 1865 on the condition that it be rung on foggy days as a warning to shipping. An initial steam foghorn was installed which was expanded to the current lighthouse, still operational. Station established 1879; present lighthouse 1914; tower 49 ft high; original Fresnel fourth order lens still in use; status active (automated).

Opposite: Heceta Head Lighthouse, north of Florence, Oregon: With its dominant position, 205 ft above sea level, the Heceta's light is the brightest on the Oregon coast, visible some 21 miles out to sea. In order to build the light on the rocky cliff, one thousand barrels of blasting powder were required to create a flat table. Station established 1894; tower 56 ft high; original and present optic first order Fresnel; status active (automated).

Previous pages: Pointe Vicente Lighthouse, Rancho Palos Verdes, California: Built in the Spanish style, this attractive lighthouse is unusual in still possessing its original third order Fresnel lens in working order. The powerful multi-prismed lens invented by Frenchman Augustin Jean Fresnel in 1822 revolutionized lighthouses around the world.
Station established; 1926; tower 67 ft high; status active (automated).

Opposite: Los Angeles Harbor Light (also known as the Angel's Gate Lighthouse), San Pedro, Los Angeles: Constructed to a unique design, this working, striped harbor or greater light is a much-loved California landmark. It was designed to hold three keepers, with the popular story being that three keepers were needed so that if two of them fought the third one could separate them.

Station established 1913; tower 69 ft high; original optic fourth order Fresnel; present optic DCB-24 solar-powered; status active (automated).

Right: Rainbow Harbor, Long Beach, California: This slender, classic-looking lighthouse is, in fact, a rarity: a brand new lighthouse, built in 2000, with much of its funding raised by a charity. Station established 2000; tower 65ft high; status active (automated).

Right: Cape Blanco Lighthouse, Curry County, Oregon: A picturesque landmark, this white, conical brick tower is Oregon's oldest continuously operating lighthouse, still working today and a popular visitor attraction.

Station established 1870; tower 59 ft high; original optic first order Fresnel; present optic second order Fresnel.

Above and opposite: Pigeon Point Lighthouse, California: This elegant wrought-iron spiral staircase, 136 steps high, is housed within the 115-ft-high tower of the Pigeon Point Lighthouse, built in 1871. The point was named in memory of the clipper ship *Carrier Pigeon,* shipwrecked on rocks nearby, following which the lighthouse was constructed. Station established 1871; tower 115 ft high; original optic first order Fresnel; present optic DCB-24; status active (automated).

Opposite: Peggy's Cove Lighthouse, Nova Scotia, Canada: Strikingly positioned among dramatic granite formations, Peggy's Cove Lighthouse is not only a frequently photographed landmark, but is also the only lighthouse in North America to double as a post office.
Station established 1868; present tower built 1915; tower 43 ft high; status active (automated).

Above: Gannet Rock, New Brunswick, Canada: The second-oldest working lighthouse in Canada, built south of Grand Maman Island in 1831, this long-standing structure was minded by Canada's most famous keeper, Walter McLoughlan, who worked here from 1853 to 1880 and whose journals offer an insight into the isolated life that the job entailed.
Station established 1831; tower 72 ft high; status active (automated).

Opposite: Oak Point Lighthouse, above St. John River, New Brunswick, Canada: A picturesque "salt shaker" tower, this is the highest light on the St. John River, built in 1902 and still active today.
Station established 1869; present tower built 1902; tower 48 ft high; status active.

Above: Old Lighthouse at Cape Spear, Newfoundland, Canada: On North America's most easterly point, Old Cape Spear was the first lighthouse to be built under the direction of the Newfoundland Lighthouse Board and stands an impressive 300 ft above sea level, guiding shipping into St. John's Harbor. In 1955 it was replaced by a new lighthouse and now operates as a visitor center.
Station established 1836; status inactive (new lighthouse established 1955).

Previous pages: Le Martre Lighthouse, Quebec, Canada: This attractive red lighthouse, guiding ships along the mighty St. Lawrence River, is Quebec's only non-automated lighthouse, operated by weights and cables. Today the lighthouse keeper's house functions as La Martre's town hall, one of many ingenious ways found by local communities to preserve their lighthouses.
Station established 1876; present tower built 1906; tower 63 ft high; status active (manned).

Opposite: Cape Tryon, Prince Edward Island, Canada: Despite being the smallest of the ten Canadian provinces, Prince Edward Island boasts a fine collection of 44 functioning lighthouses, with this square, shingled tower constructed in 1969.
Station established 1905; present tower built 1969; tower 39 ft high; status active.

Above: Harbor Head (East Quoddy Head) Lighthouse, Campobello Island, New Brunswick: Painted with the cross of St. George, Harbor Head Lighthouse is located on a separate, small islet at the north end of the Island.
Station established 1829; status active (automated).

Left: Covehead, Prince Edward Island, Canada: Housed among picturesque scenery, lighthouses, such as this pretty red-trimmed lighthouse, form a popular tourist attraction for visitors to Prince Edward Island.

Station established 1967; present lighthouse built 1976; tower 27 ft high; status active (automated).

Opposite: Big Tub Lighthouse, Tobermory, Lake Huron, Ontario, Canada: Today's reassuring lighthouse apparently traces its origins to a lantern hung by an early settler in the 1870s (one Charles Earl) to guide ships into Big Tub Harbor. The tree where the lantern was hung later became the location of the lighthouse. Station established 1885; present lighthouse 1913; tower 41 ft high; status active (automated).

Above: Amphitrite Lighthouse, Ucluelet, Vancouver Island, Canada: The coast along Vancouver Island, with its submerged rocks, steep cliffs and strong currents, is chillingly known as the "Graveyard of the Pacific." With the rise of the whaling, fishing, and lumber industries, the need for warning lights was pressing. The first lighthouse at this point was destroyed by a tidal wave in 1914, and quickly replaced with the present tiered construction.
Station established 1906; present lighthouse 1914; status active (automated).

LIGHTHOUSES OF THE
REST OF THE WORLD

Right: Gibbs Hill Lighthouse, Southampton Parish, Bermuda: Gibbs Hill Lighthouse in Bermuda is the world's oldest cast-iron lighthouse. Built on top of a tall hill, its light can be seen by ships at sea an impressive 40 miles away. In 2003 it was damaged by Hurricane Fabian, which caused the pool of mercury in which its light was suspended to spill. Thankfully it has now been renovated, with its irreplaceable 1904 lens now resting on a bed of ball bearings which allow it still to revolve.
Station established 1844; tower 117 ft high; status active (automated).

Opposite: Willemstoren Lighthouse, Island of Bonaire, Dutch Antilles: Now used as an aid to navigation, Willemstoren lighthouse was constructed in 1831 and was originally used to guide salt ships in to land.
Station established 1831; tower 69 ft high; status active (automated).

Following pages: Diamond Head, Honolulu, Hawaii: Although technically part of the United States, Hawaii's lighthouses are part of the Pacific Islands' heritage. At the eastern end of Wakiki Beach, Diamond Head is today a picturesque attraction. Its evocative name comes from the fact that sailors in the 1820s thought they had found diamonds in the volcano's slope, actually clear calcite crystals.
Station established 1899; current tower 1917; tower 57 ft high; status active (automated).

Opposite: Castillo del Morro lighthouse, Havana, Cuba: The imposing tower of this lighthouse is a familiar landmark of Havana Harbor. It stands in the Castillo del Morro, a formidable fortification built to defend Cuba, and replaces an earlier lighthouse, destroyed by the British in 1762 in an assault upon the fort.
Present tower built 1845; tower 82 ft high; status active.

Above: La Serena, Chile: Chile's long, dangerous coastline, which is over 2500 miles long, is protected by a number of lighthouses, among them La Serena, with its striking castle-like appearance. The Chilean navy actively maintains its historic lighthouses and is still building new lighthouses to this very day.
Station established 1950; tower 82 ft high; status active.

Right: Islotes Les Eclaireurs Lighthouse near Ushuaia in Argentina: This small, cheerful lighthouse, dwarfed by the snow-capped mountains behind it, stands in the Beagle Channel (named after the ship that naturalist Charles Darwin voyaged on) and marks the approach to Ushuaia, the southernmost permanently inhabited town in the world.

166

Opposite: Puerto San Juan, Puerto Rico: Puerto Rico's oldest light station boasts a unique and beautiful Moorish-style tower, built on the battlements of El Morro fort, guarding the entrance to San Juan Harbor.
Station established 1846; present tower built 1908; tower 51 ft high; status active.

Left: Forte da Barra Lighthouse, Salvador, Brazil: The coastal fort of Santo Antonio da Barra is a reminder of Brazil's turbulent history, with the Dutch and Portuguese fighting each other for possession of Salvador. Today, in more peaceful times, the fort contains a maritime museum and houses a still active 19th-century lighthouse.
Station established 1698; present tower built 1839; tower 128 ft high; status active.

Left: Lighthouse at Praia do Forte, Salvador, Brazil: Graceful palm trees frame Praia do Forte's sleek white lighthouse, offering guidance to local fishing boats at this picturesque Bahian coastal village.
Tower 82 ft high; status active.

Opposite: South Point Lighthouse, Barbados: The first lighthouse on the island of Barbados was originally exhibited at London's Great Exhibition of 1851 then shipped out to Barbados (at that time a British colony) and reassembled at the island's southern point. Although somewhat neglected in past years it has recently been refurbished and repainted. Station established 1852; tower 89 ft high; status active.

Right: Cabo do Sao Roque, Brazil: Brazil's long coastline has many lighthouses, among them this striking modern construction, a square skeletal tower, brightly painted in white and red.
Tower 105 ft high; status active.

Opposite: Cape Ashizuri Lighthouse, Shikoku, Japan: On the southernmost point of the Japanese island of Shikoku this pale, slender lighthouse, today in a national park, is a much-visited attraction. During the 19th century a Scottish engineer called Richard Henry Brunton (a protégé of the Stevenson family) became Japan's Chief Lighthouse Engineer, supervising the construction of over 50 lighthouses around the Japanese coast and setting up a training school. In Japan he is known to this day as the "Father of Japanese Lighthouses."

Above: Kovalum Lighthouse, Kerala, India: The lighthouse at Kovalum continues to guide local fishermen to safety as well as being a popular attraction for Kerala's beach-loving tourists. Although India's extensive coastline, which stretches for over 7000 miles, boasts a number of historic lighthouses, for a long time, these were constructed in a piece-meal, regional fashion. It was only in 1927, with the passing of the Indian Lighthouse Act, that the construction of lighthouses around the subcontinent was centralized.

Opposite: Amadee Lighthouse, Amadee Island, near Noumea, New Caledonia, South Pacific: This graceful lighthouse, dominating the small island on which it was constructed, has an intriguing history dating back to French colonial rule in the Pacific region. After many ships had been lost entering the lagoon at Noumea, a lighthouse was ordered by the French government. Constructed in Monsieur Rigolet's Paris workshop, the cast-iron lighthouse was disassembled into 1265 pieces and shipped to New Caledonia, where it was successfully reassembled. To this very day, its "twin" stands guard on the other side of the world, at Roches Douvres in France.

Station established 1865; tower 185 ft high; status active.

Above: Point Venus, Tahiti, Polynesia: At Point Venus, the historic landing site of many explorers including Captain Cook, this attractive white lighthouse was the work of Scottish engineer Thomas Stevenson, Robert Louis Stevenson's father. A famous Tahitian landmark, it was restored and extended in 1963.

Right: Cape Reinga Lighthouse, North Island New Zealand: Spectacularly located, Cape Reinga is New Zealand's best-known lighthouse. Although the tower itself is only 33 ft tall, it stands high above the waves, overlooking the Pacific to the northeast and the Tasman Sea to the northwest, and its light can be seen out at sea for 26 nautical miles.

Station established 1941; tower 33 ft high; status active (automated).

Opposite: Cape Brett Lighthouse, North Island, New Zealand: Cape Brett was the site of New Zealand's first shipwreck, when in 1808 the *Paramatta* encountered rough seas and was driven onto the rocks. Constructing the tower here was a formidable task, with the locally made cast-iron sections barged to the site then winched up 490 ft. Today the historic lighthouse is inactive, replaced by a 13 ft fiberglass tower in front of it. Station established 1910; tower 50 ft high; status historic tower inactive since 1978.

Right: Robertson's Point Lighthouse, Sydney Harbor, New South Wales, Australia: This diminutive light, a homely sight, is one of ten lighthouses guiding shipping within Sydney Harbor.
Station established 1910; tower 26 ft high; status active (automated).

Opposite: Cape du Couedic Lighthouse, Kangaroo Island, South Australia: This striking sandstone lighthouse, a historic gem with all original buildings preserved, was built after numerous lives were lost at sea in the treacherous waters around the island. Building the tower was a considerable feat, with material sent up from a jetty to the top of the cliff by a basket on a cable. For many years, this precarious means of transport was used to carry not only goods but also the keepers and their families to the lighthouse.
Station established 1909; tower 83 ft high; status active (automated).

Above: Mersey Bluff, Devonport, Tasmania, Australia: Lighthouses act as navigational aids, as well as warning of danger, with the pattern and color of their flashing lights used to differentiate between them. During the daytime, however, sailors use a "daymark" (size, shape, and markings) to recognize different lighthouses, with this elegant Tasmanian very distinctive in having vertical red stripes as its daymark.
Station established 1889; tower 51 ft high; status active (automated).

Right: Lighthouse at Cape Agulhas, South Africa: Reputedly modeled on the Pharos of Alexandria (the world's first true lighthouse), this impressive tower is one of the world's great lighthouses, built on the southernmost tip of Africa on Cape Agulhas (Cape of the Needles, named by the Portuguese navigator Bartholomew Dias). It was constructed from sandstone, which so deteriorated that the lighthouse was inactive between 1968 and 1988 but it has been restored and reactivated thanks to pressure from the local community.

Station established 1849; tower 89 ft high; status active (automated).

Opposite: Seal Point Lighthouse, Cape St. Francis, South Africa: An impressive sight, Seal Point Lighthouse on Cape St. Francis is South Africa's tallest masonry lighthouse and a national monument. With lighthouses among the country's oldest buildings, there is a new interest in promoting them to tourists, with tours and accommodation in keepers' cottages increasingly on offer.
Station established 1878; tower 92 ft high; status active (manned).

Above: Green Point Lighthouse, Cape Town, South Africa: Built in 1824, South Africa's oldest lighthouse still warns shipping to this very day. One of the many dramas it has witnessed occurred in 1966, when the *S.A. Seafarer* ran aground in front of the lighthouse. The lantern's rotating lens was stopped and the light focused on the ship in order to provide illumination for a helicopter crew to winch the crew and passengers to safety.
Station established 1824; tower 52 ft high; status active (automated).

Following pages: Lighthouse at Djerba, Tunisia: Dramatically silhouetted against a red sky, the elegant tower of Ras Taguerness Light on Djerba Island is a legacy of French colonial rule, still used as an active aid to navigation to this day.
Station established 1895; tower 160 ft high; status active.

LIGHTHOUSE BIBLIOGRAPHY

Bathurst, Bella, *The Lighthouse Stevensons*, (Flamingo, 2000)

Brown, Jackum, *Lighthouses* (Cassell Illustrated, 2005)

Crompton, Samuel Willard, *The Lighthouse Book* (Barnes and Noble Books, 1999)

Crompton, Samuel Willard, *The Ultimate Book of Lighthouses* (Saraband, 2003)

Guichard, Jean and Gast, Rene, *Lighthouses of France* (Flammarion 2002)

Guichard, Jean and Trethewey, Ken, *North Atlantic Lighthouses* (Flammarion 2002)

Jones, Ray, *The Lighthouse Encyclopedia* (The Globe Pequot Press, 2004)

Payton, Charles, Willes, Margaret and Wyndham, Samantha, *Lighthouses: Towers of the Sea* (The National Trust, 2005)

Sutton-Jons, Kenneth, *Pharos: the Lighthouse Yesterday, Today and Tomorrow* (Michael Russell Publishing Ltd, 1985)

LIGHTHOUSE REFERENCE SOURCES

Canada
Director General, Navigation Systems, Canadian Coast Guard, 200 Kent Street, 5th Floor, Ottawa, Ontario, K1A 0E6
Tel 1 613 993 0999 www.ccg-gcc.gc.ca

England, Wales and the Channel Islands
The Corporation of Trinity House, Tower Hill, London EC3N 4DH
Tel 44 207481 6900 www.trinityhouse.co.uk

France
Direction des Affaires Maritimes et des Gens de Mer, Bureau de Pharos et Balises, 3, places Fontenoy, 75015 Paris
Tel 33 1 44 49 86 81

Iceland
The Icelandic Maritime Association, Vesturvor 2, PO Box 120, IS-202 Kapavagur
Tel: 354 560 0000 www.sigling.is

Ireland
Commissioners of Irish Lights, 16, Lower Pembroke Street, Dublin 2
Tel: 353 1 662 4525 www.cil.ie

Norway
State of Environment Norway, Norwegian Pollution Control Authority, P.O. Box 8100 Dep., NO-0032 Oslo, Norway
Tel 47 22 57 34 48 www.environment.no

Scotland and the Isle of Man
The Northern Lighthouse Board, 84 George Street, Edinburgh EH2 3DA
Tel: 44 131 473 3100 www.nlb.org.uk

USA
Historian's Office, U.S. Coast Guard Headquarters, 2100 Second Street, SW, Washington DC 20593-0001
Tel: (202) 267-1394 Fax (202) 267-4309 Website www.uscg.mil/hq/g-cp/history/collect.html
email: www.uscg.mil/hq/g-cp/question/Questions.html
Maritime Heritage Progam, National Park Service, Dept. of Interior, 1849 C Street NW (NRHE-2280), Washington D.C., 20240-0001

ACKNOWLEDGMENTS

Thanks to the Icelandic Maritime Administration for their prompt response to our queries and to Jane Benn for her help.
Thank you also to Giovanni D'Angelico and John Moelwyn-Hughes at Corbis.